"I love Japanese food and I'm delighted that Chef Julia has taken the time to document these authentic recipes from her Japanese mother and share them with us. It's not always easy to find authentic Japanese recipes that are plant-based and also oil-free. Now I can easily recreate my favourite dishes like Japanese Curry, Okonomiyaki, and Gyoza without compromising on my health or values."

—Raw Chef Yin, Malaysia's raw vegan celebrity chef with five books, a cooking show and countless demos.

"Chef Julia is a culinary gem! I am continually inspired by her dedication to authenticity in her recipes, bringing a true cultural experience to the table. Learning from her has been a delight, and her work reflects a genuine passion for the art of cooking, making each dish an enriching and flavorful experience. Grateful to have Chef Julia as my guide in the kitchen!"

—Melissa Maris, Raw Food Romance

"Collaborating and learning from Julia Dunaway has been incredible. *Plant Based Japanese* particularly highlights her culinary skill entwined with her dedication to health and nutrition, loved by fans globally. Julia's online influence and her adventurous spirit showcase her commitment to health and lifelong learning, impacting a wide community beyond her kitchen. This is a wonderful book to add to everyone's collection.

—Rachel Detroit, Life Coach and Nutritionist

"Chef Julia's recipes are creative, delicious yet simple to execute by the home cook. I have had the pleasure of making many of the scrumptious recipes from Plant Based Japanese. Take delight in making Julia's recipes knowing your family and friends will enjoy them as much as you do. This cookbook makes healthy plant based Japanese food available to everyone!"

—Tami Kramer, Nutmeg Notebook, LLC

"I love C[...] food plant-b[...] become a sta[...] onigiri recipe and the okonomiyaki recipe."

—Kathy Hester, author of *The Ultimate Vegan Cookbook for Your Instant Pot* and *The Ninja Creami Dairy-Free Cookbook*

"Julia Dunaway ingeniously combines the rich traditions of Japanese cuisine with the healthful principles of whole food, plant-based cooking. Her passion for teaching and her dedication to wellness shine brightly through each recipe, offering a delicious and accessible path to health and vitality. Plant Based Japanese is a must-read for anyone seeking to enrich their culinary repertoire with dishes that are as nourishing as they are flavorful."

—Chef AJ, author of *The Secrets to Ultimate Weight Loss: A Revolutionary Approach to Conquer Cravings, Overcome Food Addiction, and Lose Weight Without Going Hungry*

PLANT-BASED JAPANESE

Chef Julia Dunaway

Published in the United States by Motina Books
Van Alstyne, Texas
www.MotinaBooks.com

ISBN: 979-8-88784-034-5 (paperback)
ISBN: 979-8-88784-035-2 (hardcover)

BISAC Categories:
COOKING/Vegetarian
COOKING/Specific Ingredients/Natural Foods

Printed in the United States

Also by Chef Julia Dunaway

Plant-Based Breakfast Favorites

Plant-Based Holiday Desserts

Plant-Based Basics

Plant Based Gourmet

Plant-Based Holiday Table

50 Recipes in 50 Days

Chef Julia 21 Day Challenge

This book is dedicated to my mother, Tamiko Abe Steele.

She was an artist in all aspects of life. I have a collection of her paintings, pottery, crocheted and knitted creations and most valuable of all, her Japanese recipes. I didn't know it at the time, but observing her cooking throughout my life inspired me to become a chef, and later to bring out the best of her Japanese dishes in my plant based Japanese versions.

INTRODUCTION

My Japanese Heritage

My mother is Japanese. She was born in Tokyo in 1925. Her father was a musician, playing shamisen (a three-string instrument similar to a guitar) in the Kabuki Theater. Her grandfather was a singer in the Kabuki Theater (drama with singing and dance) who once sang for the Emperor of Japan. When my mother was growing up, her house was filled with actors and musicians from the theater who learned how to play shamisen and sing from her father and grandfather. Her family was one of the first in Tokyo to own a motor vehicle and wear Western clothes.

During the war (World War II) my mother's house was destroyed by a firebomb in March 1945. She and her mother fled to the country to escape the continued bombings and danger in Tokyo. They were able to live in a small storage building at my aunt's friends' home. Food was scarce and money was worthless. My grandmother took her family's valuables and went to the farmers to trade them for food. Even their fine silk kimonos were hard to trade with such a shortage of food, but my grandmother was said to be very beautiful and convinced them to trade. Despite her efforts, she nearly died of malnutrition before the war ended. My mother worked nearby for the Japanese army and was able to get medical attention for her, and she survived.

After the war, around 1949, my mother met my father, Zack Steele, who was serving with the army in Tokyo. They decided to get married, even though the US government discouraged Americans from marrying Japanese. Since the US governed Japan from 1945-1952 during the occupation, they controlled how the marriages were approved. Even if approved by the government, the Japanese often would not allow them to live in Japanese neighborhoods. There was a lot of red tape to go through before they could marry and eventually, they did.

Initially my mother's parents were against their marriage, but after they got to know my father they approved. Their friends, however, "looked down" on her family for a long time because of this marriage. I found a folder of documents after my mother's death in which my father had to submit a request "for permission to marry a foreign national" and character references on my mother, stating she was not involved in subversive activities and there was no derogatory information in her background. I imagined my dignified, classy mother having to prove herself worthy of marrying a GI from Hickory, North Carolina, who was a cussing, drinking, cook supervisor in the army.

My parents lived in Japan for a short time and then were stationed in South Carolina. My mother left Japan at the age of 29, pregnant with me, to live in the Deep South. Looking back now, I imagine she was very homesick and anxious. She wasn't treated particularly well in the South. My father's family did not approve of him marrying a Japanese woman. People still used the term "Jap" and memories of Pearl Harbor were still fresh. Some restaurant and store owners let it be known that my mother was not welcome in their businesses.

It wasn't all bad. My father's family grew to love my mother and her children (my brother and me), and they taught her how to cook the food my father loved. My mother was used to eating rice, fish, soy, vegetables, and fruit, so she had a tough time adjusting to food cooked in bacon grease. She missed rice the most, and was pleased one day to hear that my grandmother had made some for her. She handed my mother the bowl of rice and it was covered in milk, sugar, and butter. My mother was so disappointed. Southern food did not agree with her and she longed for her fresh and simple Japanese food.

We eventually moved to northern California where my father was stationed at Fort Ord. There was a fairly large Japanese community there, as well as a Japanese grocery store. I remember shopping with her frequently for her special Japanese groceries such as miso, tofu, seaweed, vegetables, rice, noodles, sauces, and more. She would always buy us a box of Japanese candy wrapped in edible rice paper.

Although my mother cooked southern food for my father, my brother, and me, she would always eat her own Japanese food that the rest of us usually didn't try. I remember her eating miso soup out of a Japanese bowl with rice in a separate bowl, a dish of pickles, a plate with grilled fish and some pieces of nori (seaweed) on the side. I loved her Japanese food and always wanted to sample it.

At the age of 20, when I had joined the US Air Force, I was sent to a military base in Japan for over four years. Finally, I was able to meet my grandmother, aunt, uncle, and cousins. I fully embraced Japanese culture, sampled all the food and learned to cook so many dishes.

I lived far from my parents from the age of 19, until my mother moved to Texas in the early 1990s to live near me. I introduced her to the Fort Worth Japanese Society, so she could meet the local Japanese community. I became a member as well, but was not very active until 2010.

Before her death in 2006 my mother and I cooked many Japanese meals together. I wrote down so many of her recipes, asked her questions constantly, shopped with her at the local Asian market, ate at the local sushi bar with her, and watched her cook for her friends. I'm so thankful I had the opportunity to spend time with her. She lived with me the last six years of her life and the last meal I made for her was Japanese onigiri.

I started volunteering at the Fort Worth Japanese Society in 2010 and have been on the board since then. I do a lot of cooking for the monthly luncheons, festivals, and fund raisers. I dedicate this book to my mother, Tamiko Abe.

I'm writing this book to share my favorite Japanese recipes, transformed into plant-based versions.

Traditional Japanese Meal

Japanese food such as sushi, ramen, and Benihana style grilled dinners are not the daily fare consumed in the traditional Japanese household. It is more likely to be a traditional meal of "One Soup and Three Sides," or "Ichiju-Sansai," the healthy practice of eating a small bowl of soup, often miso soup, a bowl of rice, and three sides.

The sides vary according to the seasons and generally consist of a main protein (tofu or a bean dish in the plant-based way of eating) and a couple vegetables. Pickled vegetables are almost always a selection. For example, in the fall kabocha squash is popular, while in the spring you might see snow peas or asparagus. The practice of eating a bite of each food, followed by a sip of soup is also a way to slow down eating, especially when eating with chopsticks.

Mixing up what you're eating, bite by bite, allows for better digestion and absorption of nutrients. Fermented foods such as miso and soy sauce help the digestive system. This way of eating can also be helpful in maintaining a healthy body weight, as it encourages small portions of several satisfying dishes and discourages overeating.

Pantry Staples

Dashi: Plant based stock made from kombu (kelp) only or made with dried shiitake mushrooms and kombu. Powdered kombu stock can also be used.

Daikon: These are large white radishes used in soups, pickles, and grated for dipping sauces.

Dried Shiitake Mushrooms: These mushrooms are soaked in water to rehydrate them. The mushrooms can be used just like fresh shiitake mushrooms and soaking water can be used for stock.

Green Tea: There are many types of green tea, from Sencha to Matcha. Matcha comes in powdered form and is used for tea ceremony and Japanese sweets or in matcha lattes or smoothies.

Ginger: Pickled red ginger (beni shoga) is made from sliced fresh ginger or fresh ginger cut into strips and pickled in plum vinegar.

Gyoza Wrappers: For Japanese Gyoza, round wrappers made from wheat are used and they are labeled "gyoza wrappers." You can also make homemade gyoza wrappers.

Japanese Rice: When cooked, Japanese rice sticks together. There are short and medium grain varieties, with short grain always used for sushi. Medium grain brands, such as Nishiki, work well for everyday rice.

Kabocha: A sweet orange pumpkin simmered in soy sauce broth or used in soup. Kuri squash has a similar taste and can be substituted.

Mirin: This is a sweet cooking wine with an alcohol content of 14%.

Miso: White miso is most common for miso soup, however red miso, and awase (combination of both white and red) are also popular.

Nori: This is the pressed sheets of black seaweed used a wrapper for sushi or cut into strips or crumbled on top of food.

Ponzu Sauce: Mixture of soy sauce and lemon juice or yuzu juice.

Rice Vinegar: Both plain and seasoned, this vinegar is used in salads, sushi and many Japanese dishes. Seasoned rice vinegar has added salt and sugar.

Sake: An alcoholic beverage made from rice, sake is used for cooking and drinking.

Seaweed: Wakame seaweed is used in miso soup, salads, and with cucumbers. It needs to be rehydrated in cold water before using. Hijiki seaweed and kombu are other seaweeds used for Japanese cooking.

Sesame Seeds: These seeds come in unroasted white, roasted white, and black. Even if the label says roasted, a short period of roasting them in a medium hot skillet gives them a better taste.

Shichimi Togarishi: Seven spice blend made from sesame seeds, nori, red chili, citrus, pepper and other seeds is used to top soups and other dishes.

Shiso: Shiso leaves are used both as a garnish and as an edible ingredient, often to wrap food. The leaves are from the mint family.

Soba: Noodles made from buckwheat flour and used in soups or served cold with a dipping sauce

Soy Sauce: Shoyu comes in regular, light and dark with Tamari, the darkest sauce. Reduced sodium soy sauce cuts the sodium content by 25-37%.

Tofu: Bean curd made from soybeans, water and a natural additive to form the soy milk into curds. Tofu comes in super firm, extra firm, medium firm, soft, and silken blocks and is also available in shelf stable form.

Wasabi: Real wasabi is grated from the root of the wasabi plant. Common wasabi substitute is made from a powdered mixture of horseradish, mustard, starch and green food coloring.

Cooking Supplies and Utensils

Onigiri Mold: A plastic form used to form rice balls

Donabe Cooking Pot: A pot made from a special clay for use over an open flame to make "hot pots" or dishes with vegetables, tofu, and dipping sauces on the side.

Donabe Rice Cooker: A pot made from a special clay specially for cooking rice. The donabe rice cooker has a double lid for optimal steaming.

Rice Cooker (electric): An electric appliance made for cooking rice automatically.

Portable Butane Burner: A burner with a compartment that holds a can of butane fuel for cooking on tables or areas away from the stove.

Ginger Grater: The ceramic Japanese ginger grater allows the food to stay on the grater, allowing the collection of the ginger juice, and leaving behind the fiber.

Mandolin: A culinary utensil used for slicing and cutting julienne (matchstick) size pieces. A mandolin can cut very thin slices in large quantities.

Spider Tool: A type of skimmer in the form of a wide shallow wire mesh basket with a long handle, used for removing food from a liquid or skimming foam off when making broths.

Suribachi (Mortar and Pestle): A grinding bowl and wooden pestle used to crush ingredients such as sesame seeds. The bowl is a pottery bowl with a rough pattern on the inside, similar to a grater.

Sushi Mat: A tool used for making sushi rolls or to shape other Japanese dishes such as rolled omelets. Sushi mats are generally made from bamboo.

Drop Lid: A round lid that floats on top of the liquid in a pot while simmering food.

Miso Strainer: A mesh strainer that allows you to push the miso paste through the mesh with a pestle (wooden tool), into the pot of simmering broth, making it easier to dissolve the miso paste into the broth.

Steamer: Bamboo steamers are baskets that stack on top of each other, with a lid on top. The baskets are placed over a pot of simmering water and the steam cooks the contents of the baskets.

SAUCES AND DRESSINGS

Cashew Mayo

Tommie's Teriyaki Sauce

Master Fried Rice Sauce

Asian Dressing

Ginger Miso Dressing

Sriracha Aioli

Gomaiso
(Toasted Sesame Seeds)

Harusame Dressing

Stir-Fry Sauce

Mabo Sauce

Sesame Ponzu Dressing

Tofu Mayo

Goma Dressing

Cashew Mayo

Ingredients

1 cup raw cashews soaked in water for 1 hour and drained

1 teaspoon lemon juice

1 teaspoon rice vinegar

½ teaspoon nutritional yeast

¼ cup water

Instructions

Blend in a high speed blender until smooth.

Harusame Dressing

Ingredients

3 tablespoons rice vinegar

2 ½ tablespoons soy sauce

1 tablespoon date sugar or organic cane sugar

1 tablespoon tahini

1 teaspoon grated ginger

Instructions

Mix thoroughly.

Tommie's Teriyaki Sauce

Tommie always kept a jar of her homemade teriyaki sauce in the refrigerator.

Ingredients

½ cup mirin

½ cup soy sauce

¼ cup sugar (or any dry sweetener you prefer)

1 clove garlic

Instructions

Place ingredients in a small saucepan. Bring to a boil and simmer until reduced to a slightly thick glaze. Strain out the garlic. This sauce will keep for months in the refrigerator.

Stir-Fry Sauce

Ingredients

½ cup vegetable broth

¼ cup low sodium soy sauce

1 tablespoon tahini

1 tablespoon date syrup

2 teaspoons minced fresh ginger

3 cloves garlic, minced

½ tablespoon cornstarch

½ tablespoon white miso paste

1 teaspoon red pepper flakes

Instructions

Combine all ingredients in a jar and shake well. (Don't use a blender.)

Keeps for 5 days in the refrigerator.

Master Fried Rice Sauce

Ingredients

1 tablespoon tahini

1 teaspoon white miso paste

1 tablespoon low sodium soy sauce

¼ teaspoon red pepper flakes

1 tablespoon Sriracha (or more to taste)

1 teaspoon sesame seeds

Instructions

Mix sauce ingredients together and stir well with a flat whisk.

Mabo Sauce

Ingredients

½-1 tablespoon Touban Jian, OR ½ teaspoon red pepper flakes, or 1 tablespoon Sriracha.

(The best flavor for this dish is from the Touban Jian, however if you don't like spicy food add a small pinch of red pepper flakes instead.)

1 tablespoon white miso

1 tablespoon low sodium soy sauce

2 teaspoons tahini

1 teaspoon organic cane or date sugar

1 clove garlic, grated

1 teaspoon ginger, grated

½ teaspoon cornstarch

¾ cup water

Instructions

Mix the sauce ingredients together in a small bowl. Set aside.

Asian Dressing

Ingredients

2 tablespoons low sodium soy sauce

1 tablespoon maple syrup or date syrup

1 tablespoon rice vinegar

1 tablespoon lime juice

1 tablespoon tahini

¼ teaspoon fresh grated ginger

½ teaspoon yellow miso

¼ teaspoon red chili flakes

Instructions

Place in a jar and shake well or mix all ingredients together in a small bowl. Store in a covered container.

Sesame Ponzu Dressing

Ingredients

2-3 tablespoons soy sauce

1 tablespoon sugar

3 tablespoons rice vinegar

1 tablespoon tahini

1 tablespoon sesame seeds

1 teaspoon hot mustard (Chinese style, S & B)

Instructions

Place in a jar and shake well or mix all ingredients together in a small bowl. Store in a covered container.

Ginger Miso Dressing

Ingredients

1 piece ginger, grated

2 tablespoons miso

1 tablespoon sugar

1 tablespoon soy sauce

2 tablespoons rice vinegar

1 tablespoon tahini

1 tablespoon sesame seeds

Instructions

Place in a jar and shake well or mix all ingredients together in a small bowl. Store in a covered container.

Tofu Mayo

Ingredients

8 ounces silken tofu

1 teaspoon lemon juice

1 teaspoon rice vinegar

½ teaspoon nutritional yeast

¼ teaspoon Dijon mustard

¼ teaspoon salt

¼ teaspoon sugar

Instructions

Blend all ingredients in a high-speed blender until smooth.

Sriracha Aioli

Ingredients

1 cup raw cashews, soaked for 30 minutes or longer

⅓ cup water

2 tablespoons rice vinegar

2 tablespoons organic Sriracha

2 tablespoons apple cider vinegar or red wine vinegar

½ teaspoon tamari

Instructions

Blend all ingredients in a high-speed blender until smooth. Scrape down sides as necessary.

Goma Dressing

Ingredients

2 tablespoons Gomaiso

2-3 tablespoons rice vinegar

1 tablespoon soy sauce

1 tablespoon mirin

Grated garlic or ginger (optional; ½ teaspoon each)

Instructions

Place in a jar and shake well or mix all ingredients together in a small bowl. Store in a covered container.

Gomaiso (Toasted Sesame Seeds)

Ingredients

3 tablespoons roasted sesame seeds

½ tablespoon organic cane sugar or date sugar

½ teaspoon sea salt

Instructions

Toast the sesame seeds in a 12-inch skillet on medium heat. Be careful not to burn them by staying close by and shaking the pan from time to time.

Place the sesame seeds, about a tablespoon at a time, into a suribachi (Japanese seed grinder).

Use the wooden tool to grind the sesame seeds to a crumbled consistency, not a powder. Place them in a small bowl and continue grinding until all the seeds have been ground.

Add the sugar and salt and mix well. I always keep a small container of Gomaiso next to the spices by my stove and use them on my morning greens and on almost any Japanese dish.

SOUPS

Plant-Based Dashi

Dashi is a family of stocks, or powder, used as a base for miso soup, clear broth soup, and many simmering liquids. Dashi accentuates the umami.

Ingredients

5 cups water

1 6-inch piece kombu

4 dried shiitake mushrooms

4 scallions, all parts

1 carrot, sliced

1 tablespoon low sodium soy sauce

2 tablespoons mirin

1 teaspoon Takii (mushroom powder)

Instructions

Combine the water, kombu, mushrooms, scallions and carrot in a soup pot. Bring to a boil, reduce to simmer and cook for 15 minutes.

Remove the kombu. It can be used again. Add the soy sauce, mirin and Takii and simmer for 10 more minutes. Strain with a fine mesh strainer.

Kombu Dashi

I use this dashi for miso soup or a packet of kelp powder if I'm in a hurry. Kombu is edible kelp, and can be found in Asian grocery stores.

Ingredients

1 piece kombu (4 x 4 inches)

4 cups water

Instructions

Make some cuts in the kombu and place it in a quart jar with 4 cups of water. Let it steep for 3-4 hours at room temperature or the refrigerator overnight. Remove the kombu and the dashi (stock) is ready to use. Reserved kombu can be used in other recipes.

Miso Soup

Ingredients

5 cups water or homemade Kombu Dashi (4 cups dashi, 1 cup water)

1 teaspoon Takii (mushroom stock powder) or ground dried shiitake mushrooms and 1 teaspoon dried kelp powder

1 cup vegetables: Choose one or more:
  ½ cup thinly sliced mushrooms,
  ½ cup corn, ½ cup sliced snow peas,
  ½ cup julienne carrots,
  ½ cup cubed sweet or white potatoes
  ½ cup chopped onions,
  ½ cup sliced green beans,
  ½ cup peas,
  ½ cup diced zucchini,
  ½ cup sliced cabbage,
  ½ cup daikon radish, sliced,
  ½ cup cooked kabocha squash

1 tablespoon dried wakame seaweed, rehydrated in cold water

7 oz soft tofu (½ block), drained and cut into ½ inch cubes

3 tablespoons shiro miso (white) or a combination of red and white miso, 2 tablespoons white, 1 tablespoon red

2 scallions, white and green parts thinly sliced

Instructions

Bring the water or vegetable stock to a boil.

Add the Takii or shiitake mushroom powder, if using and the kelp powder. Add at least 1 cup of vegetables and reduce to a simmer. Cook vegetables for 3 minutes.

In the meantime, mix the 3 tablespoons of miso paste with ¼ cup of the heated stock from the pot. Add this mixture to the simmering stock and vegetables.

Add the tofu and cook for 30 seconds. Drain the wakame, (squeeze it to remove excess water and chop it into ½-inch pieces) and add it and the scallions and cook for another 30 seconds.

Remove the pot from the heat and serve. Sprinkle with more thinly sliced scallions and shichimi togarashi (7 spice pepper powder).

Miso Ball for "Instant" Miso Soup

Ingredients	Instructions
1-2 teaspoons miso paste for ¾ cup water (average size cup/bowl).	Put the miso paste in a twist of plastic wrap with a pinch of dried wakame, a pinch of finely chopped green onion, and a pinch of kelp stock granules.
	You could also add a tablespoon of finely diced tofu. Miso balls can be frozen. When ready to add, simply open the plastic wrapped ball and add it to boiled water in a coffee cup or small bowl.

Kuri Squash Soup

Homemade cashew milk makes this soup extra delicious.

Soak ½ cup raw cashews in water for 30 minutes or longer. Drain and add to a high-speed blender. Add 1 cup water and blend until smooth. If you like the cashew milk thicker use ¾ cups cashews and the same amount of water. Set aside one cup and reserve some for the garnish.

Ingredients	Instructions
2 cups vegetable stock	When all the pieces are done scrape them off the skins and place them in a large soup pot. Add the 2 cups of vegetables stock and bring to a boil. Reduce to simmer and cook for 20 minutes.
1 tablespoon mirin	
1 tablespoon low sodium tamari	
3-4 garlic cloves, minced	After 20 minutes place the squash in a high-speed blender, in two batches, and blend until smooth.
1 cup chopped yellow onion	
1 cup thick cashew milk	
1 ½ teaspoons grated fresh ginger	Rinse out the soup pot and place the blended squash mixture back into the pot.
1 teaspoon red chili powder (I used Chimayo chili powder)	Add the tamari, mirin, chili powder, salt and cashew milk. Mix well.
½ teaspoon kosher salt	Serve with sliced Fresno Chilis, and a drizzle of cashew milk. If the soup is too thick add more vegetable broth to thin it.
Fresno chili for garnish	
Reserved cashew milk for garnish	Variation: Add 1 tablespoon red curry paste (or yellow curry paste)

JAPANESE RICE

Japanese Rice Cooker

Brown Sushi Rice

Onigiri

Stovetop

Classic White Sushi Rice

Tofu Musubi
(Hawaiian Style Onigiri)

I use Hitomebore or Nishiki brands but any short grain or medium Japanese rice works.

Japanese Rice Cooker

To cook your Japanese rice or sushi rice, start with 3 cups rice and rinse well. Drain in a strainer for 10 minutes. Place in the rice cooker or a pot and add 3 ¼ cups of water or fill to indicator in rice cooker. Soak the rice for 15-20 minutes. Cook according to rice cooker instructions.

Stovetop

If using a regular pot, place the rinsed and drained rice in a medium pot and add 3 ¼ cups of water. Let the rice soak for 20 minutes. Bring to a boil and reduce to medium heat. Cook uncovered, until the water is nearly absorbed by the rice, about 10 minutes. Reduce the heat, cover the pot with the lid, and cook for another 10 minutes. If the rice looks a little dry, sprinkle a small amount of warm water and cook for a couple more minutes.

Brown Sushi Rice

For brown sushi rice the rice cooker is the preferred cooking method.

In the rice cooker, cook 2 cups short grain brown rice, rinsed and drained, with 3 cups water. To make a larger batch, cook 4 cups rice and 5 ½ cups water.

If you don't have a rice cooker, cook your rice on the stove top in a medium size pot. Place 2 cups cleaned and drained rice and 4 cups of water into a pot with a lid. Bring the rice and water to a boil, reduce to low and cook for 40-45 minutes, until liquid is absorbed.

You can also cook brown sushi rice in an Instant Pot. Add the rinsed and drained rice to the Instant Pot and cook on high pressure for 27 minutes. Let pressure release naturally for 15 minutes, then release rest of the way.

Variations:

Multigrain Sushi Rice

1 ½ cups white sushi rice (short grain white rice)

1 cup mixed grain sushi rice (Nishiki 7 grain mix)

Clean the white rice and rinse the multigrain mix well. Soak for 30 minutes and cook in rice cooker or by using any of the above methods.

Mixed Grain Rice Blend

For any rice, brown or white, take out 3 tablespoons of the rice and replace it with 3 tablespoon quinoa, barley, millet, multigrain mix, or any grain you prefer, and cook using the same instructions above.

Classic White Sushi Rice

You can also take out 3 tablespoons of the white sushi rice and replace it with the above grains to have sushi rice with some whole grain component.

Rice Cooker

Cook your sushi rice: 4 cups rice, rinse well. Drain in a strainer for 10 minutes. Place in the rice cooker or a pot and add 4 cups of water. Soak the rice for 15-20 minutes. Cook according to rice cooker instructions or if using stovetop, bring to a boil, reduce to low and cook for 15-20 minutes. Reduce the heat as low as possible and simmer for 5 more minutes. turn off and let sit without lifting the lid for 15 minutes.

Stovetop

If using a regular pot, place the rice in the pot and add 3 cups of water. Let the rice soak for 20 minutes. Place the pot over medium heat and cook, uncovered, until the water is nearly absorbed by the rice, about 10 minutes. Reduce the heat, cover the pot with the lid, and cook for another 10 minutes. If the rice looks a little dry, sprinkle a small amount of warm water and cook for a couple more minutes.

To prepare sushi rice, make the Sushi Rice Vinegar if you don't have the Seasoned Rice Vinegar with the orange cap or label that says it has added sugar and salt. The unseasoned rice vinegar usually has a green cap.

5 tablespoons rice vinegar

1 ½ teaspoons sea salt

2 tablespoons sugar

Mix the vinegar, salt and sugar together until sugar and salt is dissolved.

Transfer the hot rice to a large sheet pan or wooden bowl. Pour the vinegar mixture over the rice, working a small area at a time. Cut through the rice to break it up without smashing it. Fan the rice with a fan for 30 seconds. Let the rice rest covered with a moist towel. Don't refrigerate the rice or it will become hard.

Onigiri

Onigiri can be any size you like, from ⅓ cup to over ½ cup of rice each. For 3 rice balls, you need 1 cup of freshly cooked Japanese-style rice and 1 sheet of nori seaweed, cut into 3 cm (2 inch) wide strips. Allow ⅓ to ½ cooked rice per onigiri, so plan accordingly if you want to make several.

I use Nishiki, Hitomebore, or Tamanashiki brands.

You can also take out 3 tablespoons of the white rice and replace it with a grain mix, to have a white rice with some whole grain component.

Ingredients

⅓ cup hot Japanese rice per onigiri

Finely ground sea salt

Fillings:
    Simmered seasoned mushrooms
    Pickled plum (umeboshi)
    Chopped pickles (tsukemono)
    Tsukudani (konbu)
    Various tidbits such as Sesame Ginger Tofu

Instructions

Plastic Wrap Method

Using a spoon or rice paddle, lightly mix the salt into the hot cooked rice in a bowl or the rice cooker pot. Use ½ teaspoon fine sea salt for every 1 ½ cups hot rice.

Line a small bowl with plastic wrap. Put ½ portion of rice into the plastic lined bowl. Add the filling, if using. Add the other half of the rice. Gather the ends of the plastic wrap around the rice and twist them tightly.

Form the rice ball by pressing over the plastic with your hands and into a round, triangle or oval shape.

A triangle is the classic shape. Remove the plastic wrap. Wrap each onigiri with a strip of nori seaweed.

Bare Hands Method

Wet your impeccably clean hands with cold water and sprinkle them with salt. Take ½ of the rice and place on one hand. Make a dent in the middle of the rice with your other hand. Put in about 1 tsp or so worth of filling in the dent. Working rapidly, wrap the rice around the filling, and form into a ball. To make the traditional triangular shape, cup your hand sharply to form each corner, and keep turning it until you are happy with the shape. Practice makes perfect. Wrap the rice ball with 1-2 strips of nori seaweed. Repeat for the rest of the rice.

To bring along on picnic or in your lunchbox, wrap in plastic film or in a bamboo leaf (which is traditional). Some people prefer to carry the nori strips separately, and to wrap them around the onigiri when eating, to preserve the crisp texture of the seaweed.

Tofu Musubi
(Hawaiian Style Onigiri)

You will need a Musubi mold to make this dish. They are sold in Asian stores. It looks like a plastic rectangle with a lid that fits inside. This recipe makes 12 Musubi.

Ingredients

Nori (seaweed) squares

1 ½ cup Japanese rice, cooked

1 tablespoon mirin

For each Musubi

A heaping ⅓ cup cooked Japanese rice

1 piece of tofu,

⅓ piece of nori

Tofu

1 block extra firm tofu, drained and pressed and cut into 8 equal pieces

¼ cup low sodium soy sauce

1 teaspoon rice vinegar

1 tablespoon maple syrup

1 teaspoon onion powder

1 clove garlic, minced

1 tablespoon tahini

2 teaspoons tomato paste

Instructions

Mix the marinade ingredients together and add to tofu slices in a shallow container.

Marinate for 30 minutes to one hour. Bake in an air-fryer at 350° for 7 minutes, check it to make sure it's not over browning and bake 3 more minutes if it's still light colored. If it's already done, lower the heat to 300° and bake 3 more minutes. You can also use a conventional oven and bake at 375° on a parchment lined baking pan for 25-30 minutes.

Brush with low sodium soy sauce or teriyaki sauce.

Make Japanese Rice and allow to cool slightly. Place the musubi mold on a piece of plastic wrap. Add a heaping ⅓ cup of rice. Press the rice down with the musubi mold press until it's very tightly packed. Remove the mold and top with a slice of tofu. Wrap a piece of nori over the tofu and rice, sealing it in the back. Brush the exposed edges of the tofu with teriyaki sauce.

Tofu Musubi tastes best when freshly made. Assemble it right before you eat it.

SALADS

Plant-Based Miso Corn Kale Salad

Japanese Potato Salad

Cucumber Sunomono
(Pickled Cucumbers)

My Daily Greens (Blanched Greens)

Hijiki Seaweed Salad

Plant-Based Miso Corn Kale Salad

This recipe makes 6 servings.

Ingredients	Instructions
Corn (frozen is fine or fresh if you can get it) 1 ½ cups cooked corn, cooled	Mix the dressing ingredients together with a whisk.
½ cup cooked edamame (optional)	Mix the dressing with the kale, corn, and other ingredients. Top with toasted sunflower seeds, pepitas or hemp seeds and cranberries.
4-6 cups raw kale, washed and dried and cut into small pieces	
1 small red bell pepper, diced into ¼ inch pieces	
1 small carrot, grated	
½ cup red onion, chopped	
¼ cup red cabbage, shredded finely	
¼ cup shredded zucchini (optional) sunflower, pepita or hemp seeds for garnish	
Dried cranberries for garnish	

Dressing

2 tablespoons white or yellow miso paste

1 ½ tablespoons tahini

1 ½ tablespoons maple syrup

1 tablespoon tamari

2 tablespoons rice vinegar, apple cider vinegar or lemon juice

¼ teaspoon ground coriander

Dash of cayenne powder (optional)

Freshly ground black pepper, to taste

My Daily Greens (Blanched Greens)

I enjoy blanched greens at least once a day – sometimes even more frequently.

This recipe is very easy. All you need are greens and a large pot of water.

- One 10-ounce package or bag of mixed greens such as spinach, chard, and baby kale.
- Large pot of boiling water

Place the contents of the bag in the boiling water and cook it for 30 seconds. Remove to a bowl of ice water using a slotted spoon or spider tool. Drain in a colander. Squeeze all the water out of the greens. Serve the greens with a little vinegar and sesame seeds or Eden Shake sprinkle.

Japanese Potato Salad

This recipe makes 2 servings.

Ingredients

2 medium potatoes

1 small carrot

½ hothouse cucumber

2 tablespoon cashew mayo

1 tablespoon rice vinegar

Salt & pepper to taste

Instructions

Slice the cucumber thinly with a mandolin. Sprinkle with a little salt and massage with your hands.

Wash the potatoes.

Cut the potatoes into ½ inch pieces.

Cut the carrots into rounds and then cut the rounds in half.

Boil the potatoes and carrots in a small pan of boiling water until tender.

In a small bowl, add the potatoes, carrots, cucumbers slices and the cashew mayo. Mix gently.

Season with a little rice vinegar, salt and pepper.

Hijiki Seaweed Salad

Ingredients

½ cup dried hijiki seaweed

1 recipe for Sesame Ginger Tofu

1 carrot, sliced into matchstick pieces

⅓ cup shelled edamame (frozen, placed in bowl and covered with boiling water for 5 minutes)

2 cups homemade plant-based dashi (recipe in soup section)

Or 2 cups water mixed with 1 teaspoon Takii powder and ½ teaspoon kelp powder)

3 tablespoons low sodium soy sauce

2 tablespoons mirin

1 ½ tablespoons organic cane sugar or date sugar

Instructions

Soak hijiki in 4 cups of water for 30 minutes. Drain and wash under cold water. Place in a pot of boiling water and boil for 3 minutes.

In a 12-inch skillet over medium high heat, add the carrots pieces.

Cook for a couple minutes, add a tablespoon of water, if needed. Add the drained hijiki and dashi and bring it to a boil. Add the soy sauce, mirin, and sugar and reduce to medium-low.

Cook for 20 minutes. Add the edamame and a couple pieces of the Sesame Ginger Tofu, cut into small cubes. Cook it a little longer to reduce the liquid until there is very little left.

Keep for 4 days in the refrigerator and can be frozen.

Cucumber Sunomono (Pickled Cucumbers)

This recipe makes 2 – 4 servings.

Ingredients

3 Japanese cucumbers (typically very thin with no seeds)

¼ teaspoon salt

3 tablespoons rice vinegar

1 tablespoon sugar

¼ teaspoon soy sauce

1 teaspoon sesame seeds

Instructions

Slice cucumbers as thin as possible using a mandolin. Sprinkle them with salt and wait for 15-20 minutes for water to be released. Squeeze out water. Add other ingredients and mix well.

NOODLE DISHES

Sesame Noodles

Japanese Glass Noodle Salad
(Harusame)

Rice Ramen Noodle Bowls

Hiyashi Chuka Soba

Sesame Noodles

This recipe makes 4 servings

Ingredients

Dressing/Marinade

2 tablespoons low sodium soy sauce or soy substitute (coconut aminos, etc.)

1 tablespoon tahini

2 tablespoon rice vinegar

2 teaspoons date syrup

1 teaspoon Sriracha or ½ teaspoon red chili flakes

½ teaspoon grated ginger

1 tablespoon lime juice

Noodles and Toppings

8 ounces whole wheat noodles or any noodle of your choice, including zoodles or sweet potato noodles (cooked)

½ cup shelled and cooked edamame

½ cup carrots, cut into matchstick pieces

3 scallions, finely chopped

Instructions

Cook the noodles according to package directions.

Measure 1 cup of noodles and place them in a bowl.

Dress them lightly with a tablespoon of the dressing.

On a plate, place a few noodles, some of each of the vegetables and tofu, more noodles, and layer until you've used the cup of noodles, making sure to use some of all the vegetables, tofu and edamame in each serving. Drizzle more dressing as desired, and top with almonds, cilantro and extra hot sauce.

Ingredients

½ cup blanched, drained, and squeezed dried greens

½ cup red bell pepper, cut into matchstick pieces

1-2 Fresno or jalapeño peppers, thinly sliced

¼ cup roasted peanuts or roasted sliced almonds

¼ cup fresh cilantro, chopped

8 ounces Sesame Ginger Tofu

Rice Ramen Noodle Bowls

Ingredients

10 ounces Rice Ramen noodles (Lotus Foods has a selection of flavors and I used black ramen for this recipe.)

Sesame Ginger Tofu, sliced and cut into cubes

4 cups cabbage, Napa or green, sliced

8 ounces shiitake mushrooms, sliced

½ red bell pepper, cut into matchstick pieces

½ large onion, sliced

½ cup shredded carrots

Sauce

2 tablespoons red or white miso paste

2 tablespoons Tommie's teriyaki sauce

3-4 scallions, thinly sliced

Sriracha to taste

Instructions

In a 12-inch skillet, over medium high heat, sauté the vegetables, starting with the cabbage. Add the mushrooms, bell peppers and onions, cooking all the vegetables until they are tender crisp, about 5-7 minutes, add a little water if they stick to the pan. In the meantime, cook the noodles.

In a large pot of boiling water add the noodles. Boil for 5 minutes or until they are cooked to the desired texture. Remove the noodles with a spider tool or slotted spoon or tongs and place in serving bowls or in a large serving bowl. Save the noodle water.

Cover the noodles with the cooked vegetables and tofu cubes. Mix the miso paste and teriyaki sauce with about 1 ½ cups of reserved noodle water and ladle this mixture over the noodles, tofu and vegetables. Garnish with scallions and drizzle with Sriracha.

PAGE 54 – NOODLE DISHES

Japanese Glass Noodle Salad (Harusame)

This recipe makes 4 servings.

Ingredients

1 (4.2 oz) package glass noodles (potato starch mung bean noodles, such as Orchid brand)

½ of a large English cucumber, thinly sliced and then sliced into julienne pieces

1 carrot, cut into julienne with julienne peeler or knife

Other vegetables that can be added:

> Purple cabbage, finely shredded on a mandolin (½ cup)
>
> Bean sprouts (rinsed and drained, ½ cup)
>
> Crispy air fried shallots, (2 shallots, very thinly sliced, cooked for 5 minutes at 350°)
>
> Scallions, thinly sliced (about 3)

Salt for sprinkling on vegetables

8 ounces sesame ginger tofu cooked in air fryer at 375° for 15 minutes, drizzled with teriyaki sauce (optional)

2 teaspoon roasted sesame seeds

Instructions

Cook the noodles in boiling water for 3 minutes. Drain in a colander and rinse with cold water. Cut into shorter lengths with kitchen scissors. Top with desired vegetables and dressing.

Dressing

3 tablespoons rice vinegar

2 ½ tablespoons soy sauce

1 tablespoon date sugar or organic cane sugar

1 tablespoon tahini

1 teaspoon grated ginger

Hiyashi Chuka Soba

This recipe makes 3 servings. Use 9 ounces dry ramen noodles or 18 ounces fresh ramen noodles per person, cooked according to package directions and chilled in ice water to cool. You can also use any variety of Lotus Foods Rice Ramen. Follow the cooking instructions. Drain the water and rinse the noodles, then drain again and place on serving plates.

Ingredients

Toppings

8 ounces fresh shiitake mushrooms, sliced thin

2 carrots, cut into matchstick pieces (⅛ inch by 2 inches)

2 Japanese cucumbers (or ½ English cucumber) cut into matchstick pieces

3-4 scallions, thinly sliced

3-4 chives, thinly sliced

2 ears of corn, cooked, cut off the cob

6 cherry tomatoes, cut in half

2 tablespoons Japanese pickled ginger

Japanese nori, thinly sliced or packaged type that is already shredded (optional)

Toasted white sesame seeds

Chinese Karashi mustard powder (comes in a can), made into a paste by adding water

Sesame Ginger Tofu

Instructions

Simmered Mushrooms

Heat a large skillet over medium high heat. Add the sliced mushrooms and cook until they begin to release their moisture, about 3-5 minutes. Add a tablespoon or two of water to keep them from sticking. Add 2 tablespoons low sodium soy sauce and a teaspoon of organic cane sugar. Cook the mushrooms until they're soft, approximately 10-15 minutes. Set aside.

Corn on the Cob

Bring a large pot of water to a boil. Add the shucked corn. Cook for 5-7 minutes. Remove from the hot water and allow to cool. Cut the corn off the cob with a sharp knife.

Ingredients	**Instructions**

Dressing	
4 tablespoons soy sauce	Combine the dressing ingredients in a jar or bowl. Chill in the refrigerator until ready to use.
3 tablespoons sugar (organic cane sugar)	
3-4 tablespoons rice vinegar	
1 tablespoon toasted white sesame seeds	
¼ teaspoon grated fresh ginger	
1 tablespoon roasted sesame oil (or 1 tablespoon tahini for those who don't use oil)	

Assemble by placing the drained noodles on a shallow platter. Top in sections with all the ingredients kept in their own area. Drizzle with dressing and serve.

MAIN DISHES

Basic Japanese Tofu Bowl with Rice

Hibachi Fried Rice
(Harusame)

Plant-Based Japanese Curry

Loaded Japanese Sweet Potatoes

Okonomiyaki

Master Fried Rice with
Grilled Tofu Skewers

Stir-Fried Vegetables and
Tofu Vegetables

Gyoza Dumplings

Japanese Crunch Bowl

Basic Japanese Tofu Bowl with Rice

This recipe makes 4 servings

Ingredients

2 cups cooked rice

1 recipe for Sesame Ginger Tofu (See recipe below.)

½ cup shredded carrots

½ cup cucumbers

½ cup cooked green beans, greens, snow peas, peas, broccoli, or other leftover vegetables (optional)

3-4 scallions, thinly sliced

1 avocado, diced

1 jalapeño, thinly sliced

Tommie's Teriyaki Sauce and Sriracha, to taste

Nori (seaweed) squares

Instructions

Cut the Sesame Ginger tofu into small pieces.

Air fry at 350° for 5-7 minutes or place in a 400° oven for 10 minutes to crisp them up a bit.

In four serving bowls add ½ cup rice. Place the tofu and vegetables on top of the rice.

Garnish with avocados, scallions, jalapeño slices and drizzle with teriyaki sauce and Sriracha.

Master Fried Rice with Grilled Tofu Skewers

Ingredients

2 ½ cups cooked brown rice

1 cup diced onion

1 garlic clove, minced (optional)

2 cups of fresh vegetables such as:

4 cremini mushrooms, sliced

1 carrot, diced

½ zucchini, diced

½ red bell pepper, diced

1 Fresno chili pepper, sliced

¼ cup shelled edamame, frozen (Place frozen edamame in a bowl and cover with boiling water for 5 minutes, drain.)

Garnish - 2 scallions, thinly sliced for garnish, Furikake, Shichimi Togarashi, Roasted Sesame Seeds

Instructions

Mix sauce ingredients together and stir well with a flat whisk.

In a large skillet over medium high heat, add the mushrooms and cook until they're lightly browned, about 3 minutes.

Add the onions and garlic and cook for a couple more minutes. Add the other vegetables and cook for a couple minutes.

Add 2 tablespoons of water or vegetable stock, cover with a lid and cook for 3 minutes.

Remove the lid, add rice and sauce and mix well. Cook until the rice is hot, just a minute or two.

Serve with 2 **Grilled Sesame Ginger Tofu Skewers** and sprinkle with sesame seeds, Furikake, Shichimi Togarashi and scallions.

Ingredients

Master Fried Rice Sauce

1 tablespoon tahini

1 teaspoon white miso paste

1 tablespoon low sodium soy sauce

¼ teaspoon red pepper flakes

1 tablespoon Sriracha (or more to taste)

1 teaspoon sesame seeds

Sesame Ginger Tofu

Hibachi Fried Rice

Ingredients

2 ½ cups cooked brown rice

1 cup diced onion

½ cup diced carrots

½ cup green peas

½ cup diced red bell peppers

3 scallions, thinly sliced

2 tablespoons tamari

1 tablespoon tahini

½ teaspoon onion powder

½ teaspoon garlic powder

1 tablespoon rice vinegar

Freshly ground black pepper

Instructions

In a 12-inch skillet over medium high heat, cook the diced onions, carrot, and bell peppers until softened, adding 1-2 tablespoons water or vegetable stock. Cover with a lid for a couple minutes.

Add the defrosted green peas, tahini, and brown rice. Cook until rice is heated through. Add the tamari, onion powder and garlic powder, rice vinegar and black pepper. Garnish with thinly sliced scallions, Gomaiso, and shredded nori seaweed. Sprinkle with a little Shichimi Togarashi.

Stir-Fried Vegetables and Tofu

Ingredients

1 cup sliced onions

1 jalapeño pepper, thinly sliced

2 small carrots, cut into ¼-inch half-moons

1 small zucchini, cut into ¼-inch half-moons

1 small Japanese Ichiban eggplant, cut into ¼- inch half-moons

2 sides of a small bell pepper, cut into thin julienne strips, cut into 1-inch pieces

1 cup sliced shiitake mushrooms; stems removed

1 cup Napa cabbage, cut into 1-inch pieces or bok choy

2 garlic cloves, minced

2 teaspoons fresh ginger, minced

1 recipe for Sesame Ginger Tofu, prepared ahead

1 cup sauce

2 cups Japanese rice, prepared ahead, or any type of noodles

Instructions

Use 2 large shallow skillets for this recipe. Mine are Hexclad, 12 inch skillets.

Heat the first skillet over medium-high heat. When it's hot, add the onions and stir-fry for a couple minutes, until they start to brown. Add the jalapeño pepper and bell peppers and a little vegetable broth. Cover with a lid for 2 minutes. Remove these vegetables to a large bowl.

In the meantime, while the onion mixture is cooking, add the carrots, zucchini, and eggplant to the second skillet and use the same method. Sauté for a couple minutes, add some broth, and cover for a couple minutes. Remove to the bowl with the onions. Add the cabbage to a heated skillet and cook for a couple minutes, adding a little vegetable broth to keep it from sticking. Place all the cooked vegetables in one skillet. Add 1 cup of sauce and heat everything through. At the end, add the tofu, reserving some for topping.

Place a scoop of rice in a bowl, add ¼ of the stir fry, more tofu, and garnish of choice. Use noodles instead of rice if you prefer.

Ingredients	Instructions
Sauce	Combine all ingredients in a jar and shake well. (Don't use a blender.)
½ cup vegetable broth	
¼ cup low sodium soy sauce	Keeps for 5 days in the refrigerator
1 tablespoon tahini	
1 tablespoon date syrup	
2 teaspoons minced fresh ginger	
3 cloves garlic, minced	
½ tablespoon cornstarch	
½ tablespoon white miso paste	
1 teaspoon red pepper flakes	
Garnish	
Chopped fresh cilantro	
2 scallions, thinly sliced	
Sliced jalapeño or Fresno chilis	

Plant-Based Japanese Curry

The Japanese curry I ate growing up was made with a packaged curry roux. I didn't care for it. As a young adult, living in Japan, I discovered that I enjoyed the local Japanese curry rice. It's all about the curry roux! The best one I've made was with the curry spice blend by Sonoko Sakai. She sells it on her website. I also love the Japanese S & B Curry Powder. It can be found at local Asian markets or on Amazon.

4 servings

Ingredients

1 small onion or half of a large onion, chopped

2 minced garlic cloves

1 tablespoon minced ginger (grated)

2-3 sliced carrots

3-4 small Yukon gold potatoes, cut into 1 inch pieces

1 red or yellow bell pepper, cut into ½ inch pieces (optional)

1 medium size eggplant, cut into quarters and steamed for 5 minutes, then cut into 1 inch pieces before adding to the curry pot

2 tablespoons crushed tomatoes (or tomato sauce)

1 teaspoon coconut nectar or date syrup

2 tablespoon sake

1 tablespoon soy sauce or tamari

Sesame Ginger Tofu, cut into cubes

Instructions

Heat a large pan over medium high heat. Add the onions, ginger and garlic cook until they are softened, about 5-8 minutes.

Add the other vegetables along with the stock. Add the tomatoes, nectar, sake, and tamari or soy sauce.

Bring to a boil and simmer for 30 minutes. It will be rather thin so thicken it with a slurry.

Mix 1 tablespoon of cornstarch with 2 tablespoons of water in a small bowl. Add to the pot of curry and allow it to cook until it thickens.

Add the Sesame Ginger Tofu cubes. Serve with Japanese rice and pickled vegetables.

Ingredients	Instructions
5-6 white mushrooms (or cremini)	
4 cups vegetable stock	
2 tablespoons S & B oriental curry powder or your favorite curry powder such as Sonoko Sakai Curry Spice Kit	
Salt and pepper to taste	

Gyoza Dumplings

Some of my best memories are of my Japanese mother making gyoza. She panfried hers and then steamed them. I've found that the gyoza dumplings taste fine steamed instead of fried, however you can pan steam them in a skillet if you wish.

2 dozen dumplings

Ingredients

Filling

3 cups finely chopped Napa cabbage

6 ounces fresh shiitake mushrooms, sliced and chopped

3 tablespoons chopped scallions

1 teaspoon minced ginger

1 teaspoon minced garlic

¼ teaspoon cane sugar

¼ teaspoon salt

¼ teaspoon pepper

1 tablespoon sake

¼ cup finely minced carrots

1 tablespoon low-sodium soy sauce

4 ounces cubed Sesame Ginger Tofu

1 teaspoon cornstarch dissolved in 1 tablespoon water

Instructions

Heat a large skillet over medium high heat. Add the cabbage, carrots, scallions and mushrooms and cook for 2 minutes. Add the garlic and ginger. If it starts to stick add 1 tablespoon of water. Add the tofu, soy sauce, salt, pepper, sugar and sake. Add another tablespoon of water and cover the pan for 2-3 minutes. Add the cornstarch water and stir to combine. Remove from the heat and place in a bowl. Cool the filing before using.

Fill the dumpling wrapper with 1 tablespoon of filling in the center of the wrapper. Lightly wet the edge of the wrapper and fold it in half but don't seal the edge yet. Start making folds (pleats) from right to left, but only on the front side of the wrapper, keeping the back side flat. Press the folds (pleats) against the back of the wrapper to seal. Set the dumpling on the cutting board and press lightly so it sits upright. Curve it to resemble a crescent.

Ingredients

24 dumpling wrappers. (I used Gyoza/Potsticker wrappers, frozen)

Dipping sauce made from 3 tablespoons low sodium soy sauce, 2 tablespoons rice vinegar and a sprinkle of red chili flakes

Chinese Hot Mustard (optional)

Instructions

Place finished dumplings on a parchment lined baking sheet and cover lightly with plastic wrap while you're making the

dumplings. Use right away, refrigerate for a few hours, or freeze.

To cook, heat a steamer pot with a few inches of boiling water. Line the steamer insert with a perforated parchment round. Place dumplings, seam side up, on the sheet leaving 1 inch between the dumplings and the pot. Don't allow the dumplings to touch one another. Steam for 8 minutes.

Alternately, pan steam the dumplings by heating a 12-inch skillet over medium high heat. Place a single layer of dumplings in the pan and allow them to lightly brown on the bottom. Add ¼ cup of water and cover the skillet with a lid. Pansteam the dumplings for 3-4 minutes. Open the lid and allow the rest of the water to evaporate. Serve with sauce.

Loaded Japanese Sweet Potatoes

Preheat oven to 400°

4 Japanese sweet potatoes

Japanese sweet potatoes are purple on the outside and light yellow on the inside. They have a fluffy texture and are not as dense as orange sweet potatoes.

Use white potatoes, Jersey (Hanna) yams, Garnet sweet potatoes, or any potatoes you like if you can't find Japanese sweet potatoes.

Ingredients	Instructions
4 Japanese sweet potatoes	Wash the sweet potatoes and poke them with a fork in a couple places. Place the sweet potatoes on a parchment covered baking sheet and bake for approximately one hour or until a thin bladed knife can pierce the center of the potato easily. Large potatoes can take longer.

Sauce

Ingredients	Instructions
2 tablespoons mirin	
1 tablespoon miso	Mix the mirin, miso, soy sauce, tahini and ginger and set aside.
2 tablespoons low sodium soy sauce	
1 tablespoon tahini	

Toppings

1 cup shelled edamame, cooked

1 cup red cabbage, shredded

4 scallions, thinly sliced

2 carrots, cut into julienne pieces (2 inches by ⅛)

½ red onion, finely diced

2 teaspoons freshly toasted sesame seeds

Additional Toppings

Cashew cream

Tofu sour cream

Kimchi

Avocado

Shiitake mushrooms simmered in vegetable stock, soy sauce, mirin and sugar

Crispy seaweed strips

Crispy tofu

Place the frozen, shelled edamame in a bowl and cover them with boiling water for 5 minutes. After 5 minutes, drain and set aside.

Japanese Crunch Bowl

This recipe was developed to make a quick dinner using various leftovers from the recipes included in this book. I usually have Sesame Ginger Tofu, some Japanese style vegetables, fresh salad ingredients, frozen white or brown rice, and frozen edamame.

This recipe makes 2 servings.

Ingredients

1-2 cups cooked brown or white Japanese rice
4 slices Sesame Ginger Tofu
½ cup Japanese Green Beans
½ cup English or hothouse cucumbers, cut into small cubes and sprinkled lightly with sea salt
1 large or 2 medium carrots, shredded on a box grater
2 cups spring mix or salad greens
3 scallions, thinly sliced
¼ cup cherry tomatoes, cut in half
½ cup shelled edamame
¼ cup red bell pepper, diced
Toasted white or black sesame seeds

Instructions

In two shallow bowls place the spring mix, torn into small piece, add the rice, ½ cup or more per serving.

Place the tofu and vegetables on top. Drizzle with some Tommie's teriyaki sauce or Asian dressing.

Okonomiyaki

Okonomiyaki are savory pancakes filled with vegetables and in this recipe, tofu. They're served with Okonomiyaki sauce, tofu or cashew mayo, pickled ginger, and sprinkled seaweed flakes.

Commercial Okonomiyaki sauce is typically vegan. The sauces are drizzled on the pancake in lines across the whole pancake. To drizzle, place the plant-based mayo in a squeeze bottle or small plastic bag and cut off the corner.

This recipe makes 4 large pancakes.

Ingredients

8 fresh shiitake mushrooms, thinly sliced
1 ½ cups shredded green cabbage (use a box grater or knife to cut thin slices)
1 cup shredded carrots (box grater)
3 scallions, thinly sliced
1 tablespoon roasted white sesame seeds
½ teaspoon garlic powder
pinch of kosher salt
½ teaspoon fresh ginger, grated
1 cup white whole wheat flour (or okonomiyaki flour)
2 flax eggs (2 tablespoons ground flax seeds mixed with 6 tablespoons of water and allowed to stand for 10 minutes) or 6 ounces of Just Egg (mung bean egg replacer)
Up to ½ cup dashi

Sesame Ginger Tofu

Instructions

Prepare the vegetables and set aside. In a large bowl, mix the flour, garlic, ginger, and sesame seeds with flax eggs (or Just Egg) and a pinch of salt.

Add enough dashi to make a fairly thick batter. You might not use the entire amount.

Mix until just combined. If the batter seems too thin add one more flax egg. Add the cut vegetables.

On a non-stick griddle or skillet, heated to medium high heat, ladle out ¼ of the batter into a round shape. If there is room for more than one pancake at a time, ladle out more batter. In a skillet you can usually make only one pancake at a time. Sprinkle on some Sesame Ginger Tofu slices. Cook for several minutes at 325° if using an electric griddle.

Ingredients	Instructions

Toppings

Tofu or Cashew Mayo

Okonomiyaki Sauce

Pickled Ginger

Scallions

Furikake (vegan)

Shredded Nori (seaweed)

Turn over and cook for a few more minutes. It takes several minutes to cook the vegetables and for the batter to completely cook in the middle. Serve immediately with sauces and toppings.

VEGETABLES

Japanese Green Beans

Japanese Greens

Simmered Kabocha Squash

Grilled Japanese Eggplant

Glazed Japanese Sweet Potatoes

Pickled Carrots

Kale Chips

Miso Green Beans

Green Beans with Goma

Simmered Shitake or Oyster Mushrooms

Japanese Pickles

Crispy Japanese Sweet Potatoes

Jackfruit Teriyaki

Japanese Green Beans

Ingredients

8 ounces French style green beans, washed and trimmed of the stem ends

Pinch of salt

5 quarts of water

1 tablespoon tahini (I use Mighty Sesame Tahini.)

1 tablespoon low sodium soy sauce

Gomaiso to taste

Instructions

Bring the water and salt to a boil. Add the green beans.

Cook for 3 minutes and immediately remove them from the boiling water with a slotted spoon, tongs, or a spider tool and place in a bowl of ice water.

As soon as they cool down, just a few seconds, remove them from the ice water and place them in a bowl. They can still be a little warm.

Cut the green beans in half and return them to the bowl.

Drizzle with the tahini and soy sauce and toss well. Sprinkle with Gomaiso.

Miso Green Beans

Ingredients

8 ounces French style green beans, washed and trimmed of the stem ends

3 tablespoons white miso

2 tablespoons mirin

1 tablespoon maple syrup

1 teaspoon low sodium soy sauce

Roasted white sesame seeds

Instructions

Wash and trim ½ pound green beans. Fill the bottom pan of a stove top steamer with 2 inches of water. Bring to a boil. Place the green beans in the upper section and reduce the heat to medium. Steam for 5 minutes. Remove the green beans from the steamer pan and place on a large plate.

In a bowl, mix the miso, mirin and maple syrup. Add the soy sauce. Mix the sauce with the green beans and sprinkle with sesame seeds.

Japanese Greens

Ingredients

One 10-ounce package or bag of mixed greens such as spinach, chard, and baby kale or "power greens", "super-greens" as they are sometimes labeled in the grocery store.

Large pot of boiling water

½ tablespoon tahini

½ tablespoon low sodium soy sauce

Gomaiso

Instructions

Place the contents of the bag in the boiling water and cook it for 30 seconds. Remove to a bowl of ice water.

Drain in a colander. Squeeze all the water out of the greens.

Place the greens in a large bowl.

Drizzle with tahini and soy sauce and toss to combine. Sprinkle with desired amount of Gomaiso.

Green Beans with Goma (Sesame Seeds)

Ingredients

½ pound fresh green beans, trimmed and washed

1 tablespoon freshly toasted white sesame seeds

½ teaspoon sugar

¼ teaspoon salt

Gomaiso

Instructions

Prepare a bowl of ice water and set aside. Bring a pot of water to a boil and add the whole green beans. Return to a boil and cook for 1-2 minutes. They should still be tender-crisp, so don't overcook. Remove the beans from the hot water with a spider tool and immediately place them in a bowl of ice water. Drain and dry well with paper towels.

Cut them into ¼ inch pieces.

Sprinkle with desired amount of Gomaiso.

Simmered Kabocha Squash

Ingredients	Instructions

Dashi stock made ahead:

Ingredients	Instructions
5 cups water	Combine water, kombu, mushrooms, scallions and carrot in a soup pot. Bring to a boil and reduce to a simmer.
One 6-inch piece kombu	
4 dried shiitake mushrooms	Simmer for 15 minutes. Remove the kombu. Add the soy sauce, Mirin, and Takii. Simmer for 10 minutes more. Remove the mushrooms and carrots.
4 scallions	
1 carrot	
1 tablespoon low sodium soy sauce	They can be used in miso soup. Strain the stock.
1 teaspoon Takii umami powder	
2 tablespoons mirin	

For the Kabocha:

Cut around the stem of the kabocha squash and remove it. Place the knife inside the stem to start cutting it. Cut it in half, cut the half and remove all the seeds. Cut the squash into 2-inch triangles. Trim off the sharp edges.

Make a drop lid from a couple pieces of foil.

In a large soup pot add 3 cups dashi

Add a single layer of kabocha. Bring to a boil and add the drop lid. Reduce to a simmer for 10 minutes.

After 5 minutes add:

1 tablespoon organic cane sugar (optional)

2 T Mirin

After 5 more minutes add:

1 tablespoon organic cane sugar (optional)

2 tablespoon Mirin

After 5 more minutes add:

1 tablespoon sake (optional)

1 tablespoon low sodium soy sauce

½ teaspoon salt

Test Kabocha and it's ready when a chopstick easily pierces it, usually a total of 15-20 minutes. Do not overcook or it will break apart.

Simmered Shitake or Oyster Mushrooms

Ingredients and Instructions

Wash mushrooms and remove stems for shiitake mushrooms. Cut the bottoms of the oyster mushrooms. Slice the oyster mushrooms. The shiitake mushrooms can be kept whole or slice in large pieces. Place the mushrooms in a shallow pan with:

2 tablespoons soy sauce

1 tablespoon mirin

1 tablespoon cane sugar

Cook until mushrooms are soft and have absorbed the liquid. Set aside to cool.

Grilled Japanese Eggplant

Ingredients

5-6 whole Japanese eggplants

1 teaspoon fresh grated ginger

3 scallions, thinly sliced

2 tablespoon low sodium soy sauce

2 tablespoons red or white miso (optional)

1 tablespoon sake

1 tablespoon mirin

1 teaspoon roasted white sesame seeds

Instructions

Mix ginger, soy sauce, miso, sake and mirin together to form a sauce.

Preheat the oven to 400°. Place the eggplant on a baking sheet and roast in the oven for 20-30 minutes, or until it's softened and collapsed.

Alternately, use a gas or charcoal grill set on medium heat and grill the eggplant for about 15 minutes, 7-8 minutes per side.

Remove the eggplant from the oven or grill and set aside to cool. Remove skin and chop the eggplant into small pieces.

Drizzle with the sauce. Serve with scallion and sesame seeds for garnish.

Japanese Pickles

Ingredients

½ head cabbage

½ seedless cucumber

1 dried red chili pepper

1 piece kombu (1 x 3 inches)

1 teaspoon kosher salt

Toasted white sesame seed

Soy sauce

Instructions

Cut the cabbage into 1-2 inch pieces. Discard the core.

Cut the cucumber in half and peel it. Cut it in half length and then into thin diagonal slices.

Cut the dried red chili pepper into thin slices.

Toast the kombu over an open flame so it will be easier to cut.

Put all ingredients in a zip lock bag and add the salt. You can also use a Japanese pickle press.

Move the cabbage around inside the bag to soften it. Remove the air and close the bag tightly. Set in in a bowl and place a heavy object on top. Let it sit in the refrigerator for 2-3 hours. Squeeze out excess water before serving. Sprinkle them with sesame seeds and soy sauce.

This week keep for 2-3 days in the refrigerator.

Glazed Japanese Sweet Potatoes

Ingredients	Instructions
1 Japanese sweet potato, cut into ½ by 3-inch rectangles	Place the potatoes in boiling water for 3 minutes. Drain.
Glaze	Place the potatoes in the basket of an air fryer and cook at 350° for 5 minutes. Turn and cook for 3 more minutes, or until the potatoes are done.
3 tablespoons mirin	
1 tablespoon maple syrup	Coat well with the glaze

Crispy Japanese Sweet Potatoes

Ingredients

2 medium sweet potatoes

1 tablespoon cornstarch

½ teaspoon salt

2 tablespoons tahini (Mighty Sesame Tahini)

1 teaspoon salt

Instructions

Slice the sweet potatoes into sticks (like French fry size). Blanch in boiling water for 5 minutes. Drain well.

Mix the cornstarch, tahini, and salt and coat the sweet potatoes well.

Place on a parchment lined baking sheet and bake in the oven at 400° for approximately 20-25 minutes.

You can also use the air fryer at 375° for a total of 10 minutes, turning over halfway through cooking time and cooking longer, as needed.

Pickled Carrots

Ingredients

2 carrots, shaved into thin slices

½ cup rice vinegar

2 tablespoons dates sugar, date syrup, maple syrup or cane sugar

1 teaspoon salt

Instructions

Place the rice vinegar, syrup, salt and ½ cup water in a small pot. Bring to a boil and pour over the sliced carrots. Cool and drain before using.

You can also make pickled radishes or red cabbage with the same method.

Jackfruit Teriyaki

Ingredients

1 can young jackfruit, drained and rinsed, patted dry and shredded or use packaged steamed jackfruit with no oil

Tommie's Teriyaki Sauce

1 cup water

⅓ cup soy sauce or tamari

3 tablespoons maple syrup

1 tablespoon corn starch mixed with a couple tablespoons of water to create a slurry.

Instructions

Bake the jackfruit in a 400° oven on a parchment lined sheet for 20 minutes, stirring halfway through cooking time.

Bring the water, soy sauce/tamari and syrup to a boil. Add the slurry and cook for 3-5 minutes, until thickened.

After 20 minutes, mix the teriyaki sauce into the baked jackfruit. Return to the oven for 5 minutes.

Kale Chips

Ingredients

7 ounces kale leaves with stems

1 tablespoon tahini

1 teaspoon tamari

1 tablespoon nutritional yeast

2 tablespoons water

Instructions

Tear the rinsed and drained kale into large pieces. Mix dressing ingredients in bowl.

Pour the dressing onto the kale and massage the kale well.

Place the kale leaves on lined baking sheets.

Place in a 250° oven for 10 minutes, stir, and return for 10 minutes.

If not crisp, return them to the oven briefly and watch closely until they're crispy.

TOFU DISHES

Sesame Ginger Tofu

Mabo Tofu

Sesame Crusted Tofu

Tofu Soboro

Japanese Tofu Scramble

Tofu Poke Bowl

Dry Tofu Curry

Tofu Bacon

Crispy Tofu Crumbles

"Egg" Soboro

Seasoned or Smoked Tofu

Sesame Ginger Tofu

I use this tofu recipe in many of the dishes you'll find in this book.

Ingredients

1 (14 ounce) package extra firm tofu, drained and pressed

4 tablespoons low sodium soy sauce

1 tablespoon tahini

1 teaspoon grated ginger

1 teaspoon grated garlic

Instructions

Place marinade ingredients in a bowl and mix well. Slice tofu into 8 pieces and place in a glass dish or plastic bag with marinade. Marinate for 15 minutes. Bake in the air fryer at 375 degrees for 15 minutes or for 25 minutes in 375°oven. Cut into cubes or slices.

Dry Tofu Curry

Ingredients

1 (14 ounce) package extra firm tofu, drained and pressed, crumbled into ½ inch pieces or cut into cubes

½ medium yellow onion, chopped

1 teaspoon grated fresh ginger

1 cup cooked beans (pinto, garbanzo, white, pink), rinsed and drained

6 cherry tomatoes, stems removed and cut in half

½ teaspoon Organic Better Than Bouillon base or powdered vegetable stock

1 tablespoon Japanese curry powder (S & B brand)

2 tablespoons organic tomato ketchup

Instructions

Heat a large skillet over medium high heat. Add the onions and ginger and sauté for 3-4 minutes, allowing the onion to brown lightly. Add the crumbled tofu. Cook for 2-3 minutes. Add the beans, tomatoes, bouillon base, curry powder and ketchup. Cook for another couple minutes.

Serve over cooked rice, as a side dish and also use as a filling for onigiri.

Mabo Tofu

Mabo Tofu is a dish consisting of simmered tofu cubes, onions and shiitake mushrooms, sprinkled with crispy tofu crumbles, which are made ahead, and scallions, drizzled with Sriracha, and served over rice. This dish can be very spicy or very mild, depending on how you flavor the sauce.

Ingredients

1 recipe Crispy Tofu Crumbles

1 cup diced yellow onion

1 cup shiitake mushrooms, sliced

Sauce

1 cup diced yellow onion

1 cup shiitake mushrooms, sliced

1 recipe Crispy Tofu Crumbles (recipe below) optional

1 cup diced yellow onion

1 cup shiitake mushrooms, sliced

1 recipe Crispy Tofu Crumbles (recipe below) optional

1 cup diced yellow onion

1 cup shiitake mushrooms, sliced

Instructions

In a 12-inch skillet, over medium high heat, add the onions and mushrooms. Cook for a couple minutes and add ¼ cup water. Cook until water evaporates and the onions and mushrooms start to lightly brown. Add a little more water (a tablespoon) and cook until the onions and mushrooms are soft. This whole process will take about 10 minutes.

Add the tofu cubes and sauce ingredients and mix gently so as not to break up the tofu cubes. Cook until the mixture is boiling and reduce to a low simmer until everything is heated through.

At the last minute, add the Crispy Tofu Crumbles and scallions. Serve over rice, drizzled with Sriracha, if desired.

Mix the above sauce ingredients together in a small bowl. Set aside.

Tofu Bacon

Ingredients

1 14 ounce block of extra firm tofu, Cut the block of tofu in half.

For the marinade, mix together the following ingredients:

½ cup soy sauce

1 tablespoon tomato paste

2 teaspoons organic Sriracha

1 tablespoon vegan Worcestershire sauce

1 tablespoon maple or date syrup

1 tablespoon liquid smoke

1 cup water.

Instructions

For Onigirazu, use half of the block and cut large pieces about ¼ inch thick.

Cut the other half into 4 equal slabs. We'll use these for sushi rolls or burritos.

Place sliced tofu in a large shallow baking dish. Cover with marinade and marinate for 4 hours or up to overnight. Strain the tofu from the marinade and cook in a skillet or on a griddle over medium heat until browned and slightly crispy

Sesame Crusted Tofu

Ingredients

1 (14 ounce) block of extra firm tofu drained and pressed and cut into half. Cut each half into large slices, the size of the entire half, not the usual slabs

2 tablespoons ground flax seeds

4 tablespoons low sodium soy sauce

1 tablespoon rice vinegar

1 tablespoon maple syrup

1 tablespoon tahini

1 tablespoon finely grated ginger

¼ cup white whole wheat flour, rice flour or other flour of your choice

¼ cup sesame seeds (white or black or mixture of both)

Instructions

Mix flax seeds with ½ cup water and set aside. Mix soy sauce, rice vinegar, maple syrup, tahini, ginger together and marinate the tofu for 20 minutes.

Place the flour on a plate. Place the sesame seeds on another plate.

Dip each tofu slice into the flour, then the flax mixture, and lastly, into the sesame seeds. Place coated tofu pieces on a lined baking sheet or rack of an air fryer. Bake at 425 degrees for 25 minutes, turning over halfway through. For the air fryer, 375° and about 5-7 minutes per side. I had a little issue with sticking in the air fryer, so I would recommend the oven, using a parchment lined baking sheet.

Crispy Tofu Crumbles

Ingredients

1 (14 ounce) block of extra firm tofu, drained and pressed, crumbled into small pieces

4 tablespoons low-sodium soy sauce

1 tablespoon tahini

1 teaspoon grated ginger

Toppings

4 scallions, thinly sliced

Sriracha (optional)

Instructions

Mix marinade ingredients and marinate tofu at least 30 minutes. Place on a parchment lined baking sheet and bake at 400° for 30 minutes, stirring halfway through. The pieces should be very small and dark.

In a 12-inch skillet, over medium high heat, add the onions and mushrooms. Cook for a couple minutes and add ¼ cup water. Cook until water evaporates and the onions and mushrooms start to lightly brown. Add a little more water (a tablespoon) and cook until the onions and mushrooms are soft. This whole process will take about 10 minutes.

Add the tofu cubes and sauce ingredients and mix gently so as not to break up the tofu cubes. Cook until the mixture is boiling and reduce to a low simmer until everything is heated through.

At the last minute, add the Crispy Tofu Crumbles and scallions. Serve over rice, drizzled with Sriracha, if desired.

Japanese Tofu Crumbles

You'll start with one block extra-firm tofu, drained and pressed and crumbled (to press the tofu, wrap in paper towels or clean cotton cloth and place it between 2 cutting boards.

Place a heavy object, like a large book, on top of it for 15-20 minutes.

Preheat the oven to 400°

Ingredients	Instructions
4 tablespoons low sodium soy sauce	Mix ingredients together with tofu in a bowl or zip lock bag.
1 tablespoon tahini	Place tofu crumbles on a parchment paper lined baking sheet. Bake for 25-30 minutes, turning a couple times.
1 teaspoon grated fresh ginger	Bake until desired doneness. Drizzle with Tommie's teriyaki sauce, if desired.
1 teaspoon grated garlic	

Tofu Soboro

Ingredients

One block extra-firm tofu, drained and pressed and crumbled

4 tablespoons low sodium soy sauce

1 tablespoon tahini

1 teaspoon grated garlic

Instructions

Mix ingredients together with tofu in a bowl or zip lock bag.

Place tofu crumbles on a parchment paper lined baking sheet.

Bake at 375°F for 25-30 minutes, turning a couple times. Bake until desired doneness.

Drizzle with Tommie's teriyaki sauce, if desired.

"Egg" Soboro

Ingredients

1 (14 ounce) block of soft, medium, or firm tofu, blotted dry with paper towels, and crumbled

½ teaspoon turmeric (or more if desired)

½ teaspoon paprika

½ teaspoon black salt (Kala Mamak)

½ teaspoon garlic powder

½ teaspoon onion powder

Pinch of kosher salt

Instructions

In a 12-inch skillet, heated over medium high heat, add the crumbled tofu and the spices.

Cook until lightly browned, about 4-5 minutes.

Remove from the skillet and set aside.

Japanese Tofu Scramble

Ingredients

Extra firm tofu, 14-ounce block, drained and wrapped in a towel, pressed and crumbled

1 cup onion

1/2 cup cremini mushrooms or shiitake mushrooms, sliced

1 garlic clove, minced

1 teaspoon grated ginger

$\frac{1}{8}$ teaspoon (or a pinch) of ground turmeric

1 tablespoon low sodium soy sauce

2 tablespoons nutritional yeast or 2 tablespoons Fresh Jax Tofu Scramble seasoning blend

1 teaspoon fresh lemon juice

3-4 scallions, thinly sliced

1 cup baby spinach

Instructions

In a 12-inch skillet on medium high heat, add onion and cook for 3-4 minutes until it starts to brown and stick to the pan.

Add 2 tablespoons of water. Stir and add the garlic, ginger and mushrooms. Cook for 5-7 minutes until the mushrooms are softened, adding a little vegetable broth as needed to keep it from sticking to the pan.

Add the crumbled tofu, soy sauce, nutritional yeast and lemon juice. Cook for another 5 minutes, until the tofu is lightly browned.

Add the baby spinach and cook for just a minute, until it's wilted. Serve on top of rice, sprinkled with scallions and Gomaiso.

PAGE 113 – TOFU DISHES

Seasoned or Smoked Tofu

Ingredients

1 14 ounce block of extra firm tofu, drained and pressed, and sliced in ¼ inch strips.

4 tablespoons low-sodium soy sauce or any soy sauce such as smoked soy sauce (3 tablespoons low-sodium soy sauce and 1 tablespoon smoked soy sauce)

1 tablespoon tahini

1 teaspoon grated ginger

1 teaspoon grated garlic

2 teaspoons organic Sriracha

Instructions

Mix marinade ingredients and marinate tofu at least 30 minutes. Place on parchment lined baking sheet and bake at 375° for 25-30 minutes. Cut into sticks.

Tofu Poke Bowl

Ingredients

1 recipe Sesame Ginger Tofu

1 tablespoon Ogo seaweed, reconstituted in water for 5 minutes and drained, blotted dry with towel. (If you can't find Ogo seaweed use wakame seaweed, reconstituted and chopped.)

2 thinly sliced scallions

Pinch of Hawaiian salt (pink salt)

1 tablespoon tahini

1 tablespoon low sodium soy sauce

1 teaspoon grated ginger

Toasted sesame seeds

You can use a variety of toppings:
Avocado cubes

Wasabi

Shichimi Togarashi

Thinly sliced cucumbers

Sriracha

Corn

Cilantro

Instructions

Toss the ingredients gently with the baked tofu.

Place a scoop of rice in individual serving bowls. Add ¼ of the tofu to the bowl.

Top with any of the toppings and drizzle with a little teriyaki sauce.

Sushi ginger

Sliced Thai or Serrano chilies

Furikake

Macadamia Nuts or inamona nuts

Sriracha aioli (Sriracha mixed with cashew cream)

Kale (finely chopped)

Red chili flakes

SUSHI

For my plant-based sushi I prefer simple sushi rolls, both inside-out (with the rice on the outside) or with seaweed on the outside. I serve the sushi rolls with low sodium soy sauce and wasabi made from a can of powdered wasabi, made into a paste with water. Of course, if you can find true wasabi (a root vegetable), fresh grated wasabi is wonderful.

I've included a recipe for sushi ginger as well, however you can find organic, undyed sushi ginger by Ginger People and other companies.

Norimaki

Norimaki (Roll) is the basic sushi roll, with seaweed on the outside. Feel free to use one or more of the following fillings:

Tofu Bacon, Seasoned or smoked Tofu, Jackfruit Teriyaki, Crispy Sweet Potatoes, Simmered Mushrooms or Crispy Kale

The basic roll recipe Norimaki (seaweed on the outside)

- 1 cup prepared sushi rice
- 2 (8 x 8 nori sheets)

Fillings of your choice:

You can make as many different fillings as desired or you can use simple fillings such as matchstick sized pieces of cucumbers or avocado, pickled radishes, matchstick carrots or any vegetables you like.

- Tofu Bacon
- Seasoned Tofu
- Teriyaki Jackfruit
- Japanese Sweet Potatoes
- Kale Chips
- Simmered Oyster or Shiitake Mushrooms
- Sliced Avocados
- White and black sesame seeds for garnish

Place the piece of seaweed on the sushi rolling mat, shiny side down. Add about one cup of rice. Spread out the rice, leaving a 1 ½ inch border of bare seaweed. Add the strips of tofu, avocado, sweet potato, tofu and kale. Roll up tightly. You can use some mashed pieces of rice to help the bare seaweed stick to the roll. Cut into slices. Sprinkle cut rolls with sesame seeds.

Serve with low sodium soy sauce and wasabi.

Futomaki

Futomaki is a Vegetable Roll.

For this roll use one whole sheet of seaweed. The seaweed will be on the outside.

Cover the entire sheet of seaweed with rice, leaving a ½ inch border on top.

Place any or all of the following filling items on the rice:

- Strips of cucumber;
- Avocado;
- Sesame Ginger Tofu;
- Red bell pepper strips;
- Blanched greens;
- Simmered mushrooms;
- Pickled ginger;
- Lettuce at the ends with the pretty part sticking out of the roll;
- Matchbook-size strips of carrots.

Roll and place small pieces of rice on the bare seaweed to serve as "glue" to hold the roll together. Cut into 8 equal pieces.

Uramaki

Uramaki is an "inside-out roll."

The inside out roll is a sushi roll with rice on the outside like the popular California Roll. The California Roll is filled with cucumber, avocado, and crab with the rice on the outside, sprinkled with sesame seeds or fish eggs. For the plant-based version I use roasted sesame seeds on the outside.

Fillings are placed on the seaweed side and can be anything from the fillings listed below or just some avocado, cucumber, strips of seasoned tofu, Sriracha mayo, greens or anything you like.

To prepare the roll, place ½ piece of seaweed (cut the 8-inch square in half) on the rolling mat. Spread approximately ½ cup of rice over the seaweed, leaving a ½ inch border at the top. Sprinkle with roasted white or black sesame seeds. Flip the rice covered seaweed over with the uncovered strip of seaweed closest to you. Place sections of desired fillings such as jackfruit, tofu, cucumber, and avocado across the center of the seaweed. Roll away from you, tucking in the fillings and matching the seaweed strip to the seaweed behind the fillings. Use the mat to roll it until it's complete. Press lightly with the mat to even out the shape. Tuck in any fillings sticking out the ends. Cut the roll into 8 equal pieces by first cutting the roll in half, cutting each half in half, and each remaining piece in half.

Sushi Fillings

- Tofu Bacon
- Seasoned Tofu or Smoked Tofu
- Jackfruit Teriyaki
- Crispy Japanese Sweet Potatoes
- Simmered Shiitake or Oyster Mushrooms
- Kale Chips

Cashew Mayo and Tofu Mayo are great sauces for your sushi. (See Sauces and Dressings)

Other Vegetable Fillings

- Red Bell Pepper
- Carrots
- Cucumbers
- Avocado
- Lettuce (cut so the leafy part sticks out at the end)
- Blanched spinach (or mixed greens):

*Cut any vegetable into julienne strips (4 inch long, ⅛ inch wide)

Onigirazu

Onigirazu is a "sushi sandwich" in which the ingredients normally used in a sushi roll are placed in the center of a large square of seaweed (nori). The seaweed is then arranged to cover the filings to create a square bundle. The bundle is wrapped in paper or plastic wrap and cut down the center to show off the colorful fillings. You can use any ingredients you like in the onigirazu, as simple as some lettuce, tomato, sliced cucumbers and avocado, or you can make the fillings below.

Onigirazu with Sesame Crusted Tofu and Pickled Carrots

  1 cup sushi rice,

  4 pieces of 8 x 8 nori

  1 avocado, sliced

  Pickled carrots

  Sliced cucumbers

  Baby greens, such as spinach

  Sesame Crusted Tofu

  Pickled Carrots

  Sriracha Aioli

To assemble the Onigirazu: Place a sheet of nori (8 x 8) on a cutting board, rough side up. Place it in a diamond pattern. Place a handful of rice in the center, using slightly wet hands. Press the rice down to make it even. Place a layer or drained, pickled carrots, a slice of tofu drizzled with Sriracha Aioli, a few pieces of avocado, some Sriracha Aioli, a layer of spinach leaves. Some people like to add another layer of rice, but I prefer to keep it at one layer of rice, just on the bottom. Seal all four corners of the nori on top of the fillings by folding each corner over to the center. Use some grains of rice as "glue." Place a toothpick, threaded along the top in the direction you will cut the onigirazu in half because once it's wrapped it's hard to remember how you placed the inside ingredients. Wrap the onigirazu tightly in clear plastic wrap or a towel and set it aside for a few minutes before cutting to allow the nori to mold to the rice. Cut in half with a sharp knife along the direction of the toothpick.

PAGE 127 – SUSHI

Sushi Burrito

A sushi burrito is simply a large piece of seaweed (nori) filled with sushi ingredients and rolled into one large roll. Instead of slicing it, it's cut on the diagonal and eaten as a large roll. They are very handy for picnics and lunches. I had my first sushi burrito at Whole Foods Market filled with lettuce, carrots, avocado and cucumbers.

Ingredients	Instructions
Use the recipes from the basic sushi roll fillings.	Use a rolling mat, starting with a piece of nori.
1 (8 x 8) piece of nori	Place the rice on the seaweed, leaving a 2-inch border at the top. Spread evenly.
1 cup rice	
Sliced avocado	Place all the ingredients on top of the rice, lined up neatly.
Sliced cucumbers (julienne size, 2 inch by 1/8 inch thick)	Roll the roll, squeezing to keep round.
Sliced carrots, (julienne)	Cut in half on the diagonal. Serve with low sodium soy sauce and wasabi.
Sliced jalapeño peppers	
Scallions, thinly sliced in julienne	
Lettuce leaves such as green leaf	
Slices of tofu, teriyaki jackfruit or mushrooms, tofu bacon, etc.	

Homemade Pickled Sushi Ginger

Ingredients

1 cup ginger, peeled and cut into ribbons or julienne pieces

2 cups water

½-⅔ cups Ume Plum Vinegar

Instructions

Peel the ginger, cut it, and boil in water for 10 seconds. Drain the ginger. (Use the water as ginger tea.)

Cool the ginger on paper towels for 10-15 minutes.

Put it in a container with the Ume Plum Vinegar for a few hours before eating it.

Chirashi Sushi

This dish is like a sushi salad. It consists of sushi rice mixed with the Vegetable Mixture and green beans or snow peas. Add cooked, shelled edamame if you like, or cubes of Sesame Ginger Tofu.

The dish is topped with seaweed strips and pickled ginger. You can add other toppings such as cubed avocado, cherry tomatoes, cucumber slices, or any fresh vegetables you like. It makes a beautiful dish to take to a potluck or for a special occasion.

Vegetable Mixture

- 1 cup shiitake mushrooms, stems removed and sliced
- .7 ounce Kampyo (gourd strips)
- 1 carrot, cut into julienne pieces (2 inches by ⅛ inch)
- 1 cup water
- 1 teaspoon Takii (mushroom powder)
- ¼ cup sake
- 3 tablespoons Mirin
- 1 tablespoon sugar
- 2 tablespoon low sodium soy sauce

For the Kampyo, rinse it under running water and drain. In a small sauce-pan, bring water to a boil. Add the kampyo and cook for 3 minutes. Transfer to a bowl of ice water to stop further cooking. Squeeze out the water. Cut into julienne strips (2 inches by ⅛ inch).

In a small pot, over medium high heat, add the shiitake mushrooms and kampyo along with the water, Takii, sake, Mirin, sugar, and soy sauce. Simmer over medium heat and cover with a drop lid (made from aluminum foil). After simmering for about 20 minutes, add the carrots and cook for another 5 minutes. Cool the vegetable mixture completely.

Save any liquid to use in the Chirashi Sushi.

Snow Peas or Green Beans

Bring a pot of water to a boil and add the snow peas or green beans. Return to a boil and cook for 1-2 minutes. They should still be tender-crisp, so don't overcook. Remove the beans from the hot water with a spider tool and immediately place them in a bowl of ice water. Drain and dry well with paper towels. Cut them into halves or thirds.

Seaweed Strips

1 sheet nori, cut into thin strips

Pickled Ginger

Use store-bought pickled ginger such as the Ginger People (no added dyes) or make your own

Other Optional Ingredients and Toppings

- Cooked shelled edamame (Cover frozen shelled edamame with boiling water and let it stand for 5 minutes, drain)
- Japanese cucumbers, thinly sliced
- Greens (Chef Julia's Daily Greens, unseasoned)
- Cherry tomatoes
- Avocado
- Yuzu Kosho (used as a condiment)

BENTO

This recipe lists ingredients for your Bento that I recommend; however, you can use any ingredients that you like, and you don't need to use what's listed here. The combination of white rice, tofu, yellow "egg" tofu, green, orange, and red looks special and very appetizing.

You can use these bento recipes for regular plates of food or in a bento box. I have a collection of bento boxes, handy for lunches on the go. You can use meal prep containers or purchase bento boxes on-line at Amazon or Bento & Co.

Ingredients	Instructions
4 bento box containers (8 x 6 x 2 inches, single compartment)	Place ¾ cup of rice in each box.
4 servings Japanese sushi rice or Japanese medium grain rice	Lightly spread the rice to cover the entire surface of the box.
Tofu Soboro	Place the Tofu Soboro, "Egg" Soboro, Green beans and Carrots in sections on top of the rice, not mixing them up, but keeping each ingredient separate.
"Egg" Soboro	
Green Beans with Goma	
Pickled Carrots	Add a small round portion of greens, a pinch of pickled ginger, and a cherry tomato.
Pickled Ginger	
Chef Julia's Daily Greens	
Cherry Tomatoes with stem still attached	
Yuzu Kosho	

JAPANESE
BREAKFAST

A traditional Japanese breakfast consists of one soup and three dishes, just like any typical Japanese meal. Miso soup, rice, seaweed, umeboshi (plum), and Natto (fermented soybeans) are popular breakfast foods. For a plant-based Japanese breakfast try some Sesame Ginger Tofu, a bowl of white or brown rice, a bowl of miso soup, Japanese Tofu Scramble, and some Japanese style greens. Garden vegetables such as tomatoes and cucumbers can be added. It's basically a savory breakfast just like any other meal and it's so satisfying!

DESSERTS

Dorayaki

Kabocha Squash Bread

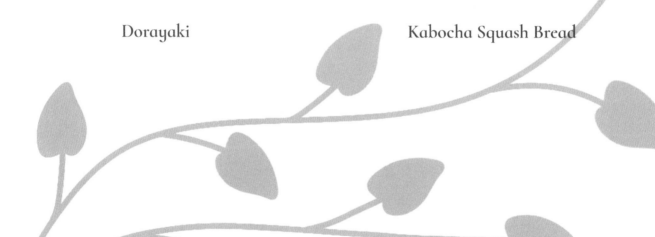

Dorayaki

Dorayaki are sweet pancakes often filled with sweet red beans. My version is whole grain and filled with a chocolate-cashew blend. These taste good with a cup of hot green tea and travel well.

Ingredients

⅓ cup silken tofu (I used Mori-Nu extra-firm silken tofu in a shelf stable box.)

¼ cup maple syrup (or date syrup)

½ cup water

1 teaspoon fresh lemon juice

2 teaspoons apple butter or apple sauce

1 teaspoon vanilla extract

1 cup whole wheat pastry flour

1 ½ teaspoons baking powder

½ teaspoon baking soda

Filling

½ cup cashew butter (or almond butter)

¼ cup maple syrup (or date syrup)

1 tablespoon cacao powder

½ teaspoon baking soda

Instructions

Place the tofu, maple syrup, lemon juice, apple butter, vanilla, flour, baking powder and baking soda in a blender. Blend until smooth, just a few seconds. Place batter in a medium size bowl and set aside for a few minutes while you make the filling.

For the filling, mix together the cashew butter, syrup, and cacao powder until smooth.

Heat an electric griddle to 300°. When the griddle is hot measure out ⅛-¼ measuring cups of batter, depending on the size you prefer. The griddle does not have to be oiled. The batter will bubble quite a bit. After 2-3 minutes, turn them over. The pancakes should be a uniform golden brown color. If they stick, use a thin spatula and gently push under the pancakes to loosen them all the way around. Cook for 1 minute and place them on a cooling rack. Alternately, use a skillet on the stovetop, however you can only cook one pancake at a time to ensure even cooking. Use medium heat and keep an eye on them so they don't burn.

Fill the cooled pancakes with the filling.

Kabocha Squash Bread

Kabocha is a lot like pumpkin. It makes a really good tasting pumpkin bread too!

Cook the kabocha by cutting it into 2-inch pieces and roasting it on a parchment lined sheet pan at 375° for 35-45 minutes, until the kabocha is soft. Remove the skin.

Ingredients

2 ½ cups whole wheat pastry flour or 2 cups whole wheat pastry flour and ½ cup almond flour

½ cup date sugar (or any dry sweetener such as organic cane sugar, maple sugar, coconut sugar)

2 ¼ teaspoons baking powder

¼ teaspoon baking soda

¼ teaspoon salt

1 teaspoon cinnamon

¼ teaspoon ginger

⅛ teaspoon nutmeg

⅛ teaspoons cloves (or 2 teaspoon pumpkin pie spice)

1 cup walnuts or pecans, coarsely chopped in large pieces, extra walnut halves for the top

3 tablespoons pepita seeds for top

1 ¼ cups cooked kabocha squash

½ cup unsweetened plant milk (soy, oat, almond)

Instructions

For the bread: preheat oven to 375°

In a medium bowl, combine the whole wheat pastry flour, dry sweetener, baking powder, baking soda, salt, spices and whisk well to combine. Set aside.

In a large bowl add the kobacha puree, soy milk, apple butter, flax egg, date syrup, and almond butter. Combine thoroughly.

Add the dry ingredients to the wet ingredients and fold together to combine well, but don't over mix or the bread with be tough. Fold in the nuts and dried fruit.

Place the batter in 4 mini loaf pans (3 by 5 ½) lined with parchment paper.

Sprinkle the top with roasted sesame seeds. Bake at 375° for 25-30 minutes, or until a toothpick inserted in the middle comes out clean.

¼ cup apple butter (Whole Foods and Amazon have sugar free brands.)

1 flax egg (1 tablespoon ground flax seeds mixed with 3 tablespoons water, left to stand for 10 minutes)

¼ cup date syrup or maple syrup

¼ cup almond butter

½ cup dried fruit (cranberries, cherries, raisins)

About the Author

Chef Julia Dunaway is passionate about teaching people that plant-based whole food cooking can be both healthy and delicious. She teaches online and in-person cooking classes, conducts intensive retreats, and maintains an active social media presence on YouTube, Facebook, and Instagram.

Her Facebook page has over 24,000 followers. She has nearly 50 on-line classes with detailed recipe packets available on her website, chef-julia.com, covering Japanese, Korean, Thai, Middle Eastern, Comfort Food, Baking, traveling and much more.

She's been on local television programs, the Chef AJ Show, podcasts, and conducts cooking demonstrations regularly in her community. She's presented at the Celebrity Chef Stage at the State Fair of Texas three times. *Plant-Based Japanese* is a collection of recipes Chef Julia developed over the years by converting the Japanese recipes she cooked for her family, many of which she learned from her Japanese mother, into whole food plant-based recipes.

INDEX

Made in the USA
Las Vegas, NV
04 May 2024

89527853R00098